# The Crane Track

## Whooping Cranes' Migration...

### *A tale of survival*

Gene Steffen

Illustrated by
Catherine Robinson

*The Crane Track: Whooping Cranes' Migration . . . A tale of survival*

Published by Wheatmark®
1760 E. River Road, Suite 145,
Tucson, Arizona 85718 U.S.A.
www.wheatmark.com

ISBN: 978-1-60494-695-6
LCCN: 2011940416

Illustrator: Catherine Robinson

*Nancy*

*Enjoy*

*Engine - Steffen*

*Dedicated to my wife,*
*Mary Kaye O'Neill*

The Whooping Cranes' Migration Route

# Contents

# Preface

Several years ago, in the course of my job as aviation manager for the U.S. Fish and Wildlife Service, I was involved in an interesting project flying near a family of whooping cranes. The National Geographic Society was filming this endangered species and developed a joint project with Canada to track their migration from the Northwest Territories in Canada to their winter home, a barrier island near Corpus Christi, Texas. At that time, there were only about 270 whoopers alive. In 1941, due to loss of habitat and hunting, only twenty-one of these great white birds were known to be alive.

I spent many hours in the air with the whoopers, a videographer from the National Geographic Society, and a Canadian biologist, who spent many decades studying these birds. We made this migration over the 2,400-mile route each way, north and south. The purpose of this project was to learn more about the birds' flight patterns, migration routes, diet, hazards, and the availability of desired habitat. During this project, which lasted several years, we learned much about these creatures and were awed by their beauty, flight characteristics, and internal homing senses. In 1984, the National Geographic Society made an hour-long video entitled *Flight of the Whooping Crane.* This was a pilot's dream to fly with the birds and with National Geographic staff on the ground.

Years later, I realized that this adventure might make a pleasurable, informative tale—fiction with real events. My idea turned out to be focused on the chick and his parents, the family, with me as the narrator. The opening chapter describes the whoopers in their wild environment, their hunting practices, and overall behavior. It includes the chick's dangerous encounter with three wolves. The next chapters cover the actual migration with absorbing vignettes along the route in respect to storms, environment, food, predators, and the chick's learning to fly formation along this route. I am not a biologist and this is not intended to be a scientific book, but rather a tale about flight and survival. Leki and his parents are part of the wild, largest flock of whoopers. Because of this and many other studies, they have brought the plight of the whooper to people's attention. Approximately 360 whoopers are in the wild and another 145 live in captivity. The total number is 513. These numbers change every year for varied reasons: predators, storms, shootings and health.

# Acknowledgments

Without the help and support of the following individuals, this book would not have come to fruition. Each provided professional expertise, support, and/or encouragement as this project came into being.

Marshall Howe
*U.S. Fish and Wildlife Service*

Ernie Kuyt
*Canadian Wildlife Service*

*Flight of the Whooping Crane*
*National Geographic*

Tom Mangelsen
*Videographer*

Tom Stehn
*Aransas National Wildlife Refuge*

Kelley Tucker
*Light Hawk*

# Introduction

This is a story about a family of whooping cranes. It is a soaring odyssey of their migration through a silent sky, their journey to a winter home. The story begins in October, in a conifer/muskeg wilderness in the Northwest Territories, Canada. The birds' migration ends about a month later on the shores of Matagorda, a Gulf of Mexico barrier island near Corpus Christi, Texas. The skyway between those two points is called the crane track, a 2,400-mile seasonal lifeline for the endangered whooping crane. These cranes are magnificent, pure white birds with jet-black feathers at the tips of an eight-foot wingspan. Leki, a whooping crane chick, is the focus of this tale.

# The Crane Track

## Whooping Cranes' Migration...

*A tale of survival*

# 1

# SUMMER ENCOUNTER

Leki saw his first wolf today, a dark shape loping along the far edge of a small lake. His parents, Toluki and Karla, were foraging in the Sass River, fifty feet to the west. Leki was standing on a marsh island, smelling and savoring the warm, sweet, Indian summer breeze from the north, as it slid southward from the big water, Great Slave Lake in Canada's Northwest Territories. He had grown confident in the air during the long days of his first summer as he flew daily with his parents. But Leki wanted to test his wings once more. He wanted to look down on that gray wolf from above, see its shape, size, and color, swoop down close to it in a long, graceful dive, bank at the last moment, and climb sharply into the clear autumn sky. Leki was at home in this sunlit Canadian wilderness, Wood Buffalo Park, the whooping cranes' nesting ground in the Northwest Territories.

Leki's mother, Karla, sensed it first—danger. She wasn't aware of how or why, but some powerful message raced across the tundra. Her skin tingled, her feathers ruffled and spread as if to catch all the electricity in the air as it transmitted information and energy. Her reaction triggered age-old instincts: fear, alertness, and protection, accompanied by an amazing keenness of vision. Toluki stood nearby, in a shallow creek, a delectable crawfish gripped in his beak. Now, a few seconds after Karla, he also became tense. Instantly, the adults called to each other, swiveling their heads toward Leki and then surveying the marsh.

Two large black wolves had crept to within thirty yards of their chick. The wolves were crouching downwind from Leki near a cluster of small fir in the opposite direction from the lone gray wolf that had captured Leki's attention. The gray wolf was the bait in an ancient hunting technique used by beast and man—distract and kill! Toluki and Karla, in their tenth year together, had observed this ritual many times. No wolf would get within fifty yards of them, but Leki had no such experience to draw on.

Still focusing on the gray wolf, Leki stretched his long neck, spread his wings, and began the series of hops that would launch him into the air. At that second, the black wolves charged. Toluki gave a warning call as he and his mate took off and wheeled toward their chick. The call startled Leki just as he was making his last hop before getting airborne. When he looked toward his parents, he saw the other wolves closing on him with startling speed. They looked gigantic and frightful at that short distance, nothing at all like the gray one some distance away. Leki was at a crucial phase in his takeoff, and distractions, especially for a young bird, could result in injury or death. His parents' warning call, together with the sight of these wolves, terrified him and short-circuited his natural flight instincts. Instead of lifting off, he stumbled at the edge of the marsh. The two wolves were just a few body-lengths away, muscles bunched for the final spring in their attack. Leki was about to feel the strength of their jaws.

Karla and Toluki, wings beating rapidly, closed the distance toward their chick. In desperation, they wheeled into a dive toward the wolves. Below, Leki was struggling to get airborne, fighting to regain a fragile balance only recently learned. One extended leg hit a raised clump of grass. He pushed off with a surge of adrenaline. Now he was over water, airborne, but wobbling badly. His right wing caught a thin pine branch, and his body canted awkwardly. Losing lift quickly, he smacked the water with a loud splash, out of control and utterly defenseless. In seconds, the wolves sprung into the water and then slowed to a stop as the firm pond bottom dropped away in the deepening water. As Leki fell into the marsh, Toluki, leading the dive, screamed downward toward the wolves. Their charge interrupted by the adult birds, and slowed in their charge, the wolves' attack churned frustratingly to an end just a few feet short of Leki. With his long legs just touching the marshy bottom and his wings flapping strongly, Leki struggled upright, slowly gathering speed, and launched himself into the air.

The frothing water slowly settled in ripples around the wolves' chests. Their wine-colored tongues, flecked with foam, hung slackly out of their mouths. They snapped their heads skyward, yellow eyes riveted on Leki as he climbed rapidly to join his parents. A breeze ruffled the small pines, and the bright sun lit this quiet piece of wilderness. The trees, tundra, marsh, and sky were nature's backdrop for a living drama—predator and prey, life and death, energy and beauty.

# 2

# LEKI LEARNS THE TERRITORY

Something was different this morning. Leki stood in the creek, head up, eyes sharp, sniffing and searching the cool, clean water for a tasty meal. The breeze ruffled his white and rose-colored feathers. He hopped from the creek up onto a tussock, stretched his neck several times, and turned slowly and deliberately in all directions. With a series of long hops and heavy, slow wing beats, he struggled into the air.

Before the sun began to create thermals and lift, his takeoff was not an easy task.

Once he got comfortably aloft, Leki climbed a hundred feet in the air. As he soared, the tundra, with its lakes, creeks, conifers, and tussock clumps, unfolded below. The orange sun, climbing slowly through the treetops, reflected moving shadows on the water. In a few minutes, the light from the sun began transforming some of the larger lakes into great rippling sheets, now appearing more like snow than water. It was a striking panorama, a mix of vivid colors in the southeastern sky.

Leki swiveled his neck, swooped, and glided, flapped, and dove, gathering speed for a sharp climbing turn above his parents. He did two more circles over his nesting site and saw Toluki and Karla looking up at him. Preparing to land, Leki pointed his beak upward for several seconds, gaining altitude. He whirled over, gathering speed, then streamlined his wings and plunged toward a small island next to his parents. Fifteen feet above the water, he spread his wings, slowing his descent. He dropped his long, skinny legs and then flared his wings for the landing. His parents watched as he touched down with one leg in a shallow pond and the other on a marsh clump. The chick was growing up, gaining confidence in the air and on the ground.

Each morning, the family would walk through their refuge looking for breakfast; it wasn't hard to find in such a rich environment. Later, with the surrounding thermals developing, they urged Leki to fly so that he'd learn the territory surrounding his nesting area and could prepare for the long migration ahead of him. Toluki, Karla, and other animals are more attuned to weather patterns than humans are. Their brains and nerves have evolved to be attuned to the physical nature of their lives. Through the summer, Leki grew stronger and flew with his parents to various parts of their park. He learned more about the dangerous animals they saw from the air and on the ground, the territory of his homeland, and flying in general.

The end of September was a few days ahead, autumn just around the corner. The terrain, food, colors, and climate were changing. Toluki, Leki, and Karla became restless.

A few days later, in midday, Leki took off alone again. He caught a thermal as he climbed and, as usual, circled around his small refuge. It was during this maneuver that his eyes swept toward the horizon and he saw a kind of sky he'd never seen. In some parts, it was a mixture of gray and purple, very dark. In other areas, snowy, pillow-like clouds full of energy, with odd, spectacular shapes, were climbing higher by the second. As he focused on one part of this spectacle, a lightning bolt slashed across the horizon, briefly forming a dramatic silhouette against the forbidding sky.

The oncoming storm was massive, part of a deepening low-pressure system shouldering its way southeastward from the Gulf of Alaska. Leki's parents, watching from below, sensed the dropping pressure and knew rain would soon enshroud them. Calling to their chick, they turned into the gusts and began their series of hops into the air. Once aloft, they joined Leki and headed south to their nesting area on a small marsh island. This island, the summer home for Leki's parents over their years together, was a safe haven, helping to protect them from wolves, fox, bobcats, and others. Surrounded by water, they could avoid surprise attacks and a flightless chick could swim to escape predators. Their nest was made of dense stands of bulrush and measured about a yard across; it truly was a refuge. It was here, amidst a rich collage of water and land, food and freedom, that Leki had been hatched months before and had learned to fly and hunt.

They flew directly toward the island, never more than three or four wingspreads above the ground, watching the ragged clouds bearing down on them. Above and to the northwest, they saw the sheets of rain, propelled by turbulent winds crossing the darkening tundra. Landing safe and secure in their nest, they watched the storm's approach. The boisterous weather was nature's messenger, announcing that winter was on its way. Change was in the air; it was the color of the falling leaves, the shorter days and frosty nights—even the fish became more elusive, seeking out their holes in the ponds and rivers.

During the furious night, as the cranes huddled in their island marsh, the temperature plummeted, the rain turned to sleet, then snow. The winds began to shift as the front sped eastward. Hours before dawn, big, moist flakes began to cloak the firs and grasses in a white mantle. The tundra began a slow transformation as the sub-arctic landscape of cedar, spruce, muskeg, marsh grass, and low shrubs became draped in its early winter 'coming-out' costume.

After the passing of this front, Leki awoke to a blinding white shroud. He was instantly alert. Four inches of snow rounded nature's rough edges. A peaceful quietness prevailed as the sun slowly rose above the horizon, casting a pink glow over the cranes' world. Leki walked, pranced, and hopped around in the snow until he reached the flowing creek. Spotting a crawfish, he stepped slowly and carefully along the bank. The crawfish didn't move. Pausing in the shade of a small spruce, which hung over the water, he extended his long neck, darted his beak into the shallow creek, and gulped down the crunchy critter.

Toluki and Karla watched their chick as he began his clumsy but effective takeoff. With no thermals or breezes at this hour, Leki flapped his wings vigorously to gain altitude. After leveling out after his climb, he looked down at his transformed playground. The dazzling snow revealed tracks of animals he didn't know existed. As he pivoted his long neck and flew a bit lower, he was able to spot rabbits, skunks, and weasels. They all acted differently, darting under cover, changing direction, staying still then bounding through the snow. Leki made a sweeping turn, his left wing well above some stunted firs. He climbed higher and began another circle. In that circle, he saw the three wolves at the edge of a pond. The memory of his close call, the vivid image of their jaws and eyes as they closed toward him, sent adrenaline streaking through his body. Fear interrupted his exploration. He wheeled around and headed back to his nest, a valuable instinct made stronger, another lesson learned.

Breezes developed as the day progressed. They strengthened into winds that spilled out of the passing low pressure system area and gave Toluki and Karla a second signal to head south. Snow had given them the first urge, though not the strongest, for an early snow was not a real threat. The other, more urgent message came from the northwesterly wind, flowing out of the fast-moving front, bending the marsh grasses, ruffling their feathers, and sending thick flakes flying horizontal over their nest. This powerful wind triggered a deep urge, not just to fly, but to spiral and soar toward their migration goal, eating up the miles on the first long hop of their journey south. A tailwind cannot be ignored, for it is part of a natural cycle, an ingredient of survival. It shortens the trip and saves energy.

Leki and his family were at their nest but not resting. They were standing tall, heads up, eyes focused on the sky and horizon. Leki could see and feel his parents' restless energy. He side-stepped over to his parents and began mimicking their actions, flapping, running, occasionally leaping into the air. Turning into the wind, Toluki and Karla began a run, followed by a series of short hops in a straight line, wings flapping strongly. Leki, about ten yards behind them, suddenly realized they were airborne, climbing quickly away. He completed his own short run and launched himself into the gusty morning air, wings beating strongly. His parents, gaining altitude, then turned their heads to make sure their chick was following. They were on their way.

# 3

# WINGING IT: THE SKYWAY SOUTH

Toluki took the lead. As he saw Leki climbing, he started a slow turn to allow him to join their formation. As Leki closed in, Karla moved back from Toluki to allow Leki to slide in between them. Now the three cranes were stacked in the safest and most efficient formation. Toluki ahead, Leki below to his right at a distance of about three wings from his dad, and Karla behind. As they climbed in a tight formation, Leki could feel the power of his parents' wings, both pushing and pulling him. They were above the tundra, climbing steadily, their wing muscles firing, climbing even higher, to just below the clouds. A half hour later, Toluki sensed the stronger winds of a thermal. He stopped flapping and adjusted his wings to take advantage of the spiral, nature's elevator that would boost them through the sky. Karla did the same; Leki fumbled a bit in the transition but quickly mimicked Toluki's movements.

The circles of their spiral enlarged their formation, and the cranes were able to spread out a bit and let the updrafts do the work. Toluki set their course southeast, his long, pointed, rust-colored beak aimed toward the Gulf of Mexico, Corpus Christi, Texas, and the Aransas National Wildlife Refuge. The whooper's strong instincts, ingrained over thousands of years, set their internal course at what humans would describe as 140 degrees. With relatively small deviations for weather, food, or a secure nesting area, they would hold this course for the next 2,400 miles.

The family settled into an energy-efficient soaring mode, eating up the miles, while gradually losing altitude. When thermals allowed, they climbed on the heated, rising air, at times up to 7,000 feet. The higher they went, the greater the tail wind and the less energy they would need to expend to cover the miles. Then, setting their wings, they resumed their glide, picking up additional speed in the descent. With strong tailwinds, they could average about forty miles per hour, or more.

Large and small ponds, enormous lakes, and winding rivers covered the region below. Leki saw another part of his home territory. The Peace River below him flowed for hundreds of miles to the southwest. Ahead and to his left, an immense body of water, Lake Athabasca, shimmered in a light blue pattern toward the horizon. Caught up in his flight formation, time and distance shrunk until Leki suddenly noticed that the hills below were becoming more distinct, the trees bigger.

The whoopers flew on over this grand country, heading southeast across the rich prairies of Alberta then into Saskatchewan, which provided perfect habitat for the migrating family. The landscape of hills, beautiful trees, grasses, and waters below were all new to Leki. The muscles, tendons, flesh, and feathers of his body were being tested as well as strengthened as he flew. His parents settled on autopilot, repeating maneuvers they'd honed to perfection. It was in these rich, golden fields of grain and pothole lakes that they would feed and nest for several days, sometimes even weeks. They'd gorge on corn, wheat, bugs, crayfish, and whatever they could find or catch, fueling up for the next part of the long flight.

As they continued to fly southward, the light seemed to soften, and the cranes glided in spirals over welcoming, beautiful lakes and fields where they would spend the night and maybe the next several days. These stopover points are special places, chosen by whooping cranes during many migrations. They are the crane's 'truck stops,' though considerably more natural and lovely than man's replicas. The prairies and pothole lakes of Alberta, Saskatchewan, and the Dakotas could be considered five-star crane hotels. For decades, farmers along the crane track have looked forward to the sound of the birds' calls, the sight of elegant flight, and their sweeping orbits as they prepared to land. The birds often return to the same farmer's fields each year.

On the first day of their migration, late in the afternoon, Toluki and his family slid down through a line of puffy, marshmallow clouds toward a resting place imprinted in his brain. The family had flown about 350 miles, a great start, but Leki's parents would instinctively shorten the day's flight until Leki became stronger. Alone, they might have flown ten or twelve hours, winds and weather permitting, but now they flew only seven or eight. This would increase as their chick's strength and technique grew. It was a challenge for Leki.

The family began circling over the Chesham Hills in the eastern part of Alberta, near the boundary of Saskatchewan. The family passed through breaks in the hills and headed for a marsh lake. Within minutes, the family was flying below some of the treetops and followed them to the lake. They saw a bear near the creek, lots of ducks, some white pelicans in the lake, and three deer standing next to the edge of trees, looking up. None of these animals were predators. Toluki picked out a landing spot on some soft ground a few feet from a marsh. Spreading their wings, like flaps on a plane, they slowed their descent and dropped their long legs, touching softly to the earth.

Water, marsh grasses, and small islands surrounded them. Food was abundant; the birds feasted on the crayfish, other crustaceans, amphibians, and small fish that thrived there. They also ate insects as well as snakes and fruit. Grain fields often touched the water's edge or were only a short flight away. Tall grasses in a marsh or on an island in the water would be their inn, protecting them from the wind and natural enemies. Varied weather conditions, including strength and direction of winds, habitats and distance to the next resting place are all ingredients in their flight south. The birds' physical condition is directly related to their goal.

One afternoon, several days after leaving their northern summer nest, the family was flying formed in a tight spiral of lift over the undulating prairies of southern Saskatchewan. Fields of ripening, golden canola spread across the low hills two thousand feet below. Leki and his parents had been riding the edge of a twenty-five-knot wind flowing southeastward from Great Slave Lake. If these winds held for a few more days, they'd soon be eating grain near some farmer's pothole in Montana or North Dakota. Almost effortlessly riding the thermals, the cranes zoomed up to several different altitudes until they tired or the clouds' streets dissipated. These weather phenomena changed every day and often changed during the day.

Rolling out of the thermal/spiral, Toluki and his family began their gliding, still pointing their beaks toward their wintering grounds, the shores of the Gulf of Mexico, two provinces and six states ahead. As they started a gliding descent, the speed over the ground increased. Leki could sense a difference in his body, almost like a push from the winds, helping them along. Suddenly, off to one side, he saw some motion and color in the sky. He looked behind at Karla and saw her gazing intently at some other birds that seemed to be flying directly at them, but his parents held their course.

The approaching birds looked much like his parents but were smaller with gray or mottled, sandy-colored feathers, sandhill cranes! The flock of about forty closed in toward Toluki, then began a graceful curve into a tight formation, melding with the whoopers. The air around Leki was filled with loud clucks and calls as the sandhill cranes joined them on their journey. Leki had never seen or been this close to other birds and had never experienced the raucous calls and humming sound of other wings surrounding him. The noise and so many bodies, so close, disoriented him. He lost his focus. His body and wings seemed out of control. With a jerk, he changed his wing set and position and began to fall away from Toluki. He then started flapping vigorously, which made his position worse and disrupted the formation. A raucous cry came from the sandhills. The chick's actions had upset their formation, and they broke quickly from their position with the whoopers.

Except for a few brief turns of their necks, Leki's parents appeared to take little notice of their new flight mates. With all the new sounds and movements surrounding him, Leki forgot some flight lessons only recently learned. His mother slid ahead and nudged him, coaxing him back in place. Toluki twisted his head, caught Leki's gaze, held it a few seconds, and turned back, intent on his task as leader. Leki's heart beat rapidly. His muscles tensed and then relaxed as he retrieved his place. With a low murmur, the sandhills rejoined them. Leki settled down, perhaps more secure, surrounded by his parents and the other friendly birds. Now, the whole flock was riding a supporting and powerful wave of air driving them toward their winter home. Leki was caught up in the focus of the journey and the great number of birds.

The sandhills flew with Leki's family for the next few days as they crossed the Saskatchewan River south of Saskatoon. Toluki flew the flock over Moose Jaw where Leki saw his first jet streak past as it climbed away from a military base. For a few seconds, he reacted to the roar of the engine by falling out of formation, but he quickly slid behind Toluki. Each day, these new sensations of the journey became imprinted forever in his brain. Near sundown, the flock soared across the U.S. border, circled the eastern Montana town of Plentywood, and flared to a landing in a lovely marsh on the edge of a wheat field. Depending on tomorrow's weather, the flock might cross the boundary into North Dakota and then over the Missouri River and the town of Williston.

The migration had fallen into a predictable pattern.

Each morning after eating and drinking close to their chosen resting place, the cranes would launch into the sky looking for developing thermals at about nine o'clock, human time. The sandhills, though greater in number, had accepted Toluki as the flock leader. They followed when Toluki made the decision to go and landed in formation as he selected a resting site each evening. The autumn weather, always unpredictable along their route, had been unusually kind to them. Mostly sunny skies, puffy, white cumulus 'cloud streets,' foretelling strong thermals, occasional thundershowers, light crosswinds, or strong tailwinds had marked their journey. They were making good time.

Several days after leaving Montana and passing through the Dakotas, the flock was enjoying an early breakfast. The fine weather had stayed with them, particularly the tailwind and thermals. Toluki soon was calling to the birds, and in a short time, he jumped and ran, leading the flock into the sky. They flapped to gain altitude, and then Toluki turned slightly toward a series of clouds, caught a thermal, and hung on as the birds spiraled high in the sky. At about three thousand feet, the winds dissipated, and the flock adjusted their wings, as they effortlessly glided on course.

Late in the afternoon, the clouds thickened, and except for a small opening toward the northeast, the sky was overcast. The thermals were gone, and the flock had to start flapping. Leki looked around to the sides, ahead, and up and down, wondering what was happening, but his place in the formation never wavered. Peering down, he saw hundreds of other sandhills heading diagonally across their path. A few minutes later, he felt changes in the air around him and watched the nine sandhills that had flown with them. They abruptly peeled away in a beautiful diving arc to join their gang and slickly merged with the larger flock beneath them. To Leki, it was like they never existed, though they had flown with them for days. He and his parents were now alone in this part of the sky. The muffled whir of their three pairs of wings was much different; Leki stayed in formation but searched the sky. The sandhills were no longer in sight, their calls and clucks gone with them, having been another experience in Leki's aerial odyssey.

The family descended to just above a river following its banks, the oxbow lakes, the ponds nearby, and the main current. Toluki was looking for a place to land and maybe find other whoopers; colors and size were easy to spy amidst the other birds. After heading along Nebraska's Platte River for several miles, Toluki seemed more focused on a farm near an oxbow lake. He circled it several times, as always, to determine if it served their needs as a stopover—water, food, and safety from predators. The cranes descended in a gentle arc and landed next to a creek that flowed into the Platte. Toluki and Karla had spent nights here at this exact place on many migrations. The farmer and his family welcomed them today, happy to see the whooper's chick. Just before nightfall, Leki gorged on crayfish. Then, comforted by the touch of his parents' feathers, he slept peacefully. Things were not so comfortable elsewhere.

Hundreds of miles away in Calgary, Canada, the temperature fell fifteen degrees amidst blowing snow. This strong, early winter storm, called an "Alberta Clipper," began sweeping through the western prairie provinces of Canada and heading southeast, the same direction the birds were going. In the opposite direction, west of Cuba, a hurricane had been chugging closer and getting stronger, toward the northwest as a developing low-pressure system sucked up the warm waters of the Gulf Stream. It was toting some surprises. In about a week or two, nature's climatic bullies, one from the north and one from south, could be dancing wildly together along the whooper's migration route.

# 4

# HALFWAY TO THE FAMILY'S REFUGE

Toluki rose early to find that the winds had picked up near the cranes' marsh area. The sky was an ominous, dirty gray, but no rain was falling from the dark clouds. A little later, Karla and Leki began wading slowly and carefully through the small stream, looking for breakfast. Leki was learning where and when to find food, whether it was in a cornfield, a pond, or a creek. Toluki had chosen a fine stopover. There was no way for the cranes to know that some 1,300 miles to the southeast, the leading edge of a weather front was dropping a gentle rain between Florida and the barrier islands off New Orleans.

Suddenly, the family heard, clear and close, calls of other whoopers. Leki saw them first; nine white cranes about a hundred feet above them, circling in a slow climb. His eyes followed the cranes' direction, but his attention was interrupted by Toluki's own call. He was high-stepping on a bit of firm ground, his beak pointed toward the flock.

Leki watched his father spring into the air and begin his climb to join the other birds. Karla called to her chick. He ran awkwardly but quickly from the water onto the firm ground and followed behind Karla to launch into the air. They were joining the other flock. Within minutes, they had joined the other whoopers and were heading southeast. Gray clouds had flattened the sky, and the twelve birds had to struggle to make headway or gain altitude. Without thermals this morning, the families began to flap their wings, expending considerable energy. The temperature was dropping, and Toluki soon realized they were fighting a headwind. The new flock's leader changed directions, trying to get some lift, but nature was not on their side this day. In a few minutes, it appeared that they were being blown back to where they had started their climb. The nine whoopers' leader tried to maintain the flock, but they scattered as the winds increased and shifted in different directions.

Quickly, Toluki veered out of the flock to keep his own family together. Some of the other birds were flying alone, recklessly, but he focused on the land below. Circling, he looked for a place where they'd find cover, water, food, and safety. He dropped lower, but the wind was still strong. There were many fields, but most were in the open without creeks or ponds. The winds pursued, and he changed his heading to the west and climbed back up. He needed height for a better view of the terrain.

Toluki and Karla had flown in these conditions before: it wasn't easy, but they'd managed. Now, with their chick, it was more difficult to maintain formation. Karla was behind and had to trail the flight maneuvers of Toluki and keep Leki behind his dad. Due to the weather and his search for a good place to land, Toluki was also tested. They were all struggling. The southeast flow was pushing them north, and Leki was tiring.

The other nine whoopers were out of sight, gone in the raging sky. His eyes and wings moving fast,

Toluki kept turning, hoping to find a landing spot. Karla and Leki were still following him, but were trailing Toluki farther apart from their usual tight formation. Finally, the dark sky broke open and the rains began. It wasn't a deluge, but the mist, along with virga, made it difficult for Toluki to see.

During the last circle to his right, Toluki had seen a small stream and two ponds. He turned and flew toward them, descending closer to the creek. Two places seemed safe to land, and he circled the area twice to choose the better one.

The family was now flying just above the trees, and Toluki noticed a thick area of small trees and bushes next to the stream. The water looked clean and shallow; varied crops surrounded the area. As he made another tight turn and began a descent over the stream for landing, he saw something furry edge out of the woods. Karla saw it also. Toluki made a circle to get back around, and there they were; two foxes, looking skyward. He saw that Leki and Karla were taking in the scene, but they'd drifted farther behind. He began to climb, then made a shallow turn to allow Karla and Leki to catch up and close the formation.

With effort, Leki and Karla fell in behind Toluki and increased their wing beats to climb. The rain got heavier. Leki was losing his focus in the formation, his wings a little out of control. Toluki saw that Karla had widened her distance behind Leki, an unusual action for her. He flew up the creek to the west as it meandered through rolling hills, woods, and farms. He saw no more foxes or other predators as the sun peeped through some clouds. He made a slow turn and saw a pond with four whoopers walking in the edge of a fresher creek. He circled the birds and went lower. He'd finally found a suitable roosting site for the rest of the day or longer, depending on the weather. The four other birds were part of the flock that had earlier scattered in the wind. Toluki's family slid into a landing formation and was on the ground in seconds. They would be able to rest and have company.

The whoopers had chosen a good roosting place. Together now, the seven birds broke the quiet prairie, calling, dancing, hopping in the air, and walking as a flock. They spent the night there and part of the next morning, eating and waiting for the winds to subside and the hot air to rise into thermals. Later in the afternoon, the rains began again. The seven birds managed to fly low, covering short distances to other feeding places in the creeks and grain fields. As the day went on, it seemed that the rough weather had slowed their surge toward their winter home. But for how long?

# 5

# COLLISION IN THE PRAIRIES

The whoopers hung around their new neighborhood, the heavy overcast sky like a blanket covering their camp. However, it was not all bad. Leki and the other birds had time to rest, rebuild their flapping power, improve their takeoff and landing skills, and gobble up the rich, plentiful food. On the third day, the birds woke to another gray, somber sky. The flock surveyed its surroundings and watched the sky. The local fields and creeks provided a varied menu of corn, mice, acorns, some snakes in the field, and crayfish, clams, fish, and frogs in the ponds.

When the feeding was over, the calls of the whoopers began. Leki watched the other birds as they danced and jumped, but it seemed to him that something was wrong. After a few minutes, the birds just walked around, their calls dwindling over the fields. They were not ready to leave, and several looked toward Toluki. Leki saw his dad in the midst of the cranes, preparing to take off amidst the other birds. In seconds, his dad was airborne, the new leader of the flock. Leki trailed, then Karla, as if pulled aloft by her mate and chick.

Leki and Karla followed closely as Toluki made a few circles around the other cranes that were still on the ground, looking up. Toluki climbed steadily, higher toward the southeast, flapping strongly toward a yellowish, sandy horizon, an unusual sky. Finally, the whoopers on the ground started to walk slowly, then danced and jumped, and in seconds were climbing to get into the formation. They quickly joined the family, but the weather was not helping their start. The clouds were low, just above the trees, and the breeze became blustery. Along with the weather, the whoopers were getting squeezed between the lowering lumpy clouds and the earth.

There was another possible problem for the flock—golden eagles. These eagles are predators that can take varied birds, including big ones like whoopers, right out of the sky. Though not common, this could happen in a kind of box, formed between a small space on the ground and the air. In this situation the whoopers aren't able to get thermals; they're forced to fly in an area, favoring an eagle's attack. It was a day for the birds to stay alert.

Instead of flying directly on course, southeast, Toluki began a wide circle, and the whoopers followed. During his turns, he found a part of the sky that might allow them to climb more steeply toward the early sun, in hopes of finding some thermals. Over the weeks of their migration, Leki had learned to react when Toluki began to turn and climb. As Leki looked back toward Karla, he also saw that the four other birds were flying farther behind and spread wide apart. When he looked around, away from the sun, he saw faint violet colors in the clouds and heard thunder. Suddenly, a giant wave in the sky engulfed them and threw the birds about. Lightning slashed across the sky. The color in the clouds changed rapidly; the sky was now a dark gray. The temperature dropped, and snow pellets began falling out of the clouds. The once-distant weather bullies from Canada and Cuba had joined up to rumble together over Nebraska.

The whoopers, including Leki's family, were sucked into the maelstrom, tossed in different directions, and were quickly out of control. Leki couldn't see any other birds or his parents as he tumbled through the sky. Large flakes of snow began to fall heavily, and his sight was completely obscured, his eyes pummeled by the strong winds and heavy snow. He was just a chick, but his survival instincts took over, helping him regain some stability. Leki had been flying well above the trees. Should he fight the weather, just ride with the buffeting winds? Something told him to descend.

Through the whirling air, Leki could barely see some trees and bushes ahead. He was able to make a small turn to his left, and then he rolled straight ahead, staying a safe distance from the woods. He saw some water and then high grass near it. Leki bounced in the sky but came down farther, flying as best he could toward the space he'd seen. He never had made a landing in such a situation and had no options, just luck. His wings were hard to manage and control, but he was able to fly closer to the trees where the winds weren't quite as wild. He made a short circle around the pond, then dropped his legs, dangled them below, very close to the shallow water, and then splashed and rolled hard to a stop. The chick was alive, but totally alone.

Leki walked slowly out of the water, cold, sore, and hungry. He didn't know where he was, or where his parents and the other whoopers were. The snow was still falling, the winds raging. He looked around to see what kind of place he was in. All he could see was a kind of pale whiteness in some directions, and a darkening sky in others. Because the storm was still violent, surrounding him, he could only see a small distance, perhaps thirty yards. Leki remembered that while he had been in the sky, he had seen high grass near the water, and now he looked for some to settle into and get out of the furious weather. Nearby, he saw a creek that fed into the pond where he had landed. Leki followed the edge of the water, looking for somewhere he could also get out of sight and out of the cold. He looked in all directions but didn't see any birds, animals, or predators. Ahead he saw a marsh with cattails and a dense stand of bulrush, now covered with snow. Maybe it was a place to roost. Fortunately, the creek was not frozen, and he high-stepped his long legs through the water, his eyes and beak busy scanning for some food.

# 6

# ALONE

This was the first time Leki had to find food without the help of his parents. He quickly caught a crayfish, crushed it with his beak, and walked up the creek, looking for more. He kept going, managing to snatch another crayfish and a frog. Then he heard a cracking sound. Leki went on high alert. He stopped walking in the creek and stretched his body and beak. It had sounded like a branch breaking, but he didn't know where. Heavy snow was still falling, blanketing the environment and muffling most sounds. Leki turned back toward the marsh and twisted his head as he walked. The windswept location was a weather war, but he made it back to his resting site. The sky was iron gray and darkening; visibility was obscured, the snow still blasting sideways through the air. The pond was out of sight, due to the hazy mist, but he could see the creek, nothing else at all. It was time to go under cover as much as he could and get some warmth. He thrashed around and hunkered into the grass as low as he could. The frog and crab dinner provided some strength. At least Leki was warm and relatively safe.

After a long sleep, Leki was aroused by the call of birds, but they weren't those of whoopers. Deep snow had covered the area where Leki had spent the night. Dawn had emerged along the eastern horizon. He was able to see the surrounding environs—trees, water, and farmland. He stood up, looked in all directions, and could hear birds flying. They sounded low, but there were clouds all around except for a slice of blue sky toward the southeast. The noise of bird calls slowly drifted away and this morning the winds were not as boisterous as yesterday.

Leki walked to the creek and found breakfast: a snake, beetles, and plants. The main storm had passed through, but parts of the weather lingered. It was still cold and snow pellets fell slowly through low clouds; it was very still. He was energized, anxious to move, but Leki had a dilemma. Should he stay and wait for his parents or try to catch up with them? How would they find him or could he find his parents? Which way would he go? Staying another day in this site might be dangerous.

Leki made a choice. In a minute, Leki walked out of the creek, looked about, found some bare ground, and began to run and jump. He flapped his wings, climbed above the trees, and circled the site slowly, mapping the pond and creek below. On the edge of the pond, close to his roosting site, there were two large, furry animals, one looking up, and the other drinking. Leki thought they were small wolves and was glad to be in the air.

He was uncertain which way to go, so he began to expand his circles to find other whoopers or sandhills either in the air or on the ground. Without any plan, he drifted toward the southwest, and on the fourth circle, he saw a creek. He flew toward it, and far to his left on the edge of a pond were two large birds. Leki climbed higher to watch them. They appeared to be fighting, but as he got closer, he realized that a golden eagle was holding down a smaller sandhill crane with his talons and was tearing at his prey's chest. Leki whirled around in the other direction to get far away. He flapped as fast as he could and hoped the eagle would not come after him. Leki looked back, and the two birds were still thrashing with the eagle still on top.

It was late morning when Leki had spotted the eagle, and now he kept his course in a southwest direction. The weather was getting warmer, and puffy clouds were developing from the south. He climbed higher for some time, still alarmed by the voracious eagle. Later, near a cloud street, Leki began to feel the bounces of thermals and remembered the smoothness of how his dad adjusted his wings. Now he was flying alone, in charge, and had forgotten about the birds fighting. He climbed in spirals for several thousand feet until the thermals dissipated and then began his gliding, going farther, faster, looking for his parents or other cranes. He kept flying in the same track and looked below to see a large body of water.

Leki had learned so much from his parents during their odyssey, and he missed them. They had taught him what to eat, which animals are predators, how to fly, and more. He followed the Arkansas, the biggest river he encountered, which makes a wide turn at a town named Great Bend in Kansas. By the look of this area, Leki thought there would be many migrating cranes landing in the nearby rivers, ponds, and creeks. He descended toward the river, and as he got close, it seemed much wider than it had from above, with trees along each side and frothy, white water tumbling like a turbulent cloud in the sky. This was something quite new and made him a little uneasy, but he flew on.

Leki had been gliding, and now he was about three hundred feet above the ground. He swiveled his head in different directions and turned to follow the river, heading toward the sun. He began flapping his wings and watched clouds forming toward the southeast. It was time to begin his spirals, his lift, so he could fly higher to find his birds, in the sky or on the earth. For a long time, Leki rode the thermals until they slipped away, then adjusted his wings for the speed of gliding and the right course. The weather was fine, and he had covered many miles.

For several hours, Leki hadn't seen any birds at all, and he'd instinctively changed his course to the south. Something in his brain and eyes told him to follow the sun, not the river, and late in the afternoon, his beak was aimed at the lowering, orange horizon. Soon, Leki would have to level off and start flapping. He'd had a long day with hard work, beautiful flying, uncertainty, and a frightening eagle sighting. He needed to find a good place to land, hopefully with some other birds, and soon. He was getting tired.

The area that Leki was flying over was much the same as other prairies he'd traversed. He was flapping over trees, farms, small rivers, and towns, bushes, ponds, and creeks. He found a narrow river ahead, and on both sides were places he could stop. Field crops, barns, cattle, and other signs of humans were scattered around the area. As he slid down to just above the trees, Leki seemed comfortable in this environment, but he hadn't forgotten the predators.

Leki picked out a creek that had no trees alongside, and it wandered through the farms and ponds. He descended about sixty feet above the water and followed its winding course. All the sharp turns he was making after a long day's flight were hard on his wings and his young body; he would have to land very soon. He swerved around another bend, and there below, on his right, he saw two whoopers and two sandhill cranes, not more than fifty yards away and walking at the edge of the pond. They hadn't seen him yet, but Leki was overjoyed. He had recognized Toluki and was flying in a circle. In seconds, all the birds glanced up. Toluki saw his chick, then splashed out of the water, ran up on some grass, jumped, and bounced up a couple times, and was in the air to join his Leki.

Leki watched Toluki fly up to him, and it seemed like he was in another world; he'd found him! Toluki smoothly slid next to his chick, and they were together. They flew around in circles, and then dove low near the two other sandhills and the other whooper. Instinctively, Leki knew Toluki would land right next to Karla. In their final approach, Leki flew closer to his dad, just a wing away, not like the spread formation the family had used during the migration. In some ways, during his lonely adventure, he had changed, and his position nearer Toluki in the sky was a symbol of his maturing.

They landed near the edge of the creek and walked fast to where the three cranes were standing. Karla was not the bird in front of him. Where was his mother? Toluki looked at his confused chick and uttered a few clucks. Leki walked beside his father, then followed him around near the water. The whooper and sandhill cranes stayed put and clucked nosily, then their calls faded away. Toluki stayed close to his chick, and they walked alone, calling low to each other, on the way to his nest for the night.

# 7

# LANDING IN THE GULF'S ISLANDS

When the morning sun rose, just above the horizon, the birds awakened. It looked like they were in for good weather and a long flight. They walked through the pond and creek to catch their breakfast and soon were ready to fly. The mixed flock included Toluki and Leki, the unknown whooper, and the two sandhill cranes. All had scattered during the fury of the raging prairie. After Leki finished his meal, he walked closer to the lone whooper again, and they exchanged calls as they walked. *Where was his mother,* Leki wondered? *Was she safe, alive?*

Toluki seemed to be the leader of these birds, and he began his jumps, and then ran to get into the air. All the birds were right behind him. Fair-weather cumulus clouds were puffing higher and looked like floating, autumn cottonwoods. These kinds of clouds are triggered or energized by thermals, and all the birds could feel it, a sweet start for the day's flight. Toluki knew the course he would take; Leki was next in the formation, followed by the three other birds. They easily slipped into their flying pattern. In a short time, Toluki and the birds stretched out their wings and caught a spiral to take them as high as it would last. As the flock settled into their elevator, they also noticed a tailwind from the northwest. If it stayed with them, the flock could make it into Texas, on the way to the gulf. They stayed with the thermals to about five thousand feet, when the clouds, the temperature, and the amount of vapor changed. The cranes slick bodies and wings leveled out and began gliding, the downhill roller coaster that fueled the migration flights.

It seemed like a long time that Leki was flying next to his dad and the other cranes. Karla was missing, but he wasn't alone anymore, and he knew his dad would find her somehow. Leki remembered the sandhill cranes and whoopers he had flown with, and now a few more had joined the family. The weather and winds provided smooth flying with this new group. Following Toluki's track, they were able to fly a long way, in the general direction of their winter home, Aransas National Wildlife Refuge and Matagorda Island.

The flock had been flying for hours, and the sun would soon begin to slide toward the horizon. Light rain ahead had begun, and far ahead the sky was darkening; it was time to find a place to feed and nest. Toluki and Karla had often stopped at farmers' crops and lands, and Toluki would know if they were close. A while back, after crossing the Red River, the boundary of Oklahoma and Texas, they had passed over Dallas. Except for Leki's flight over the Moose Jaw military base in Saskatoon, with its streaking jets, he had never seen or heard any planes. Now he heard and saw them again, flying in all directions above the huge city. Even by gliding very high, it seemed to Leki that this part of the sky was uneasy, too many planes. However, Toluki seemed calm. The other cranes made some calls and continued to follow their leader.

From experience, Toluki followed several large rivers, the Brazos, the Colorado, and many small ones, which would help him stay on track. He was aware of dozens of small towns and large cities, Houston and Austin. Also, a kind of a corridor, south and east, had become a compass in his brain.

The flock began to level off near a wide creek and just above the trees nearby. They began to flap their wings, and Toluki was leading the birds around the turns of the creek. Leki had heard some calls and clucks but hadn't seen any birds yet. On one side of the creek, he saw farms, fields of grain, ponds, and houses. He knew his dad had been here before and wondered why there were no cranes or other birds. Toluki circled the area several times to choose a good landing spot. He saw a large pond on the other side of the creek, and he focused on that. He guided the birds around in a circle and found a good place to land on the edge of the pond. Toluki dropped lower. All the birds were in formation, and they dangled their long legs, adjusted their wings, and touched down at the edge of the creek.

Some of the birds began feeding right away, others clucked, walked, and looked around. The sun was just about to disappear below the horizon, and the calls and clucks were a way to make sure all was well. Suddenly, calls were heard in the air; they were close. The flock was looking toward the sky and toward the direction of the sinking sun. In seconds, three sandhill cranes and two whooping cranes, wings sharply angled, wheeled around the bend over the creek, ready for landing. The five new birds were very low with legs down and made a tight turn, then splashed into the shallow water.

The sun had dropped below the horizon, but the sky was violet, and the birds could still see. The calmness of the surrounding area was shattered as the flocks walked toward each other, and clucks and calls livened the group. Toluki and Leki were in front of the three cranes and were about thirty feet away when they both started jumping, dancing up in the air, and the calls and clucks got more boisterous. Karla was there, back in the family. They had endured a long separation and now had found each other. They all were lucky to have lived through the horrible storm.

The family walked away from the flock and looked for dinner in a pond or creek. They were able to snatch some frogs, crabs, two small snakes, some plants, and minnows. After such a long time away from Karla, Toluki wanted to be with his reunited family, make their nest together for the night away from the seven other cranes. During the night, it rained hard for hours, but just before dawn, it stopped. There was mist over their camp and some fog, but by full sunup, the sky was changing, and it appeared that their flight to their winter home would be smooth. They would know as soon as they began their climb.

They slept longer than usual, and when they got out of their roost, the rest of the seven birds had already fed and were ready to go. Would the birds go alone or together? Did they believe the family wanted to fly separately? Only the clucks would determine. The noise began as the clucks and calls of the cranes' anticipated takeoff. Toluki called and jumped a bit while Karla and Leki also watched other cranes flap and climb in a circle over their camp. The family took its time and walked the creeks and ponds for a morning feast. This place they slept in truly was a perfect stopover.

Toluki got the family away from the water, and soon they were ready to go; it was time to get to the gulf. Favorable weather conditions were developing. The clouds to the east were puffed by mild winds from the west, and the sky was bright and clear. Toluki started his jumps and running, then was in the air with Leki and Karla trailing behind. They flapped vigorously, made their climb, and within a few minutes, the thermals and spirals took over. They were able to ride those street clouds all the way to about four thousand feet. It was a cool morning, and they glided at a speed that pushed them along at a forceful rate. Leki and his parents felt good. The weather was mild with only some light rain toward the southeast.

Hours later and three times riding the thermals and soaring long distances had helped them make amazing progress toward their destination. Out ahead, looking through the smog and fog, they could see the horizon and just barely the ocean. About one thousand feet above the ground, they were running out of that elevator, the engine that had helped them so much during their odyssey. They could see different kinds of strange objects that weren't trees, lakes, or hills. Karla and Toluki were somewhat used to these urban fixtures—buildings, streets, houses, wires, and poles; a serious problem. As they flew lower, the family got more anxious, and they began to flap their wings.

The family descended to about five hundred feet as they headed for the beaches and the sea. At last, the Gulf of Mexico! Toluki went down to two hundred feet where there were several bays and numerous islands. He and Karla had stopped there on several trips. Today, though, he was focused on Matagorda and San Jose, beautiful locations for a winter home— lots of cranes, warm weather, and varied food, in different waters.

After flying low and circling different places around the area, he chose San Jose. Whooping cranes, sandhill cranes, and all kinds of birds were there to greet them. The family was in trail formation behind Toluki, and they were turning sharply to land, their strong wings extended. They dropped their legs, made a sweet touchdown next to a shallow creek, and began to call and cluck. The family was safe, healthy, and happy, and best of all they were together. Leki had gained important survival experience during the days of being separated from his parents. The resilience of the trio had prevailed over many challenging, adverse conditions, and they had arrived safely at their traditional winter home.

Here they will stay for the next 5–6 months. Sometime in the early Spring, when the winds are just right, instinct will call them North once again and they will return to the Northwest Territories. They will travel along the same 'Crane Track' they followed to get to the Gulf. These birds are magical!

CPSIA information can be obtained at www.ICGtesting.com
Printed in the USA
LVOW041751160812

294645LV00006B/56/P